AFTER THE END:
Unwrapping Grief

David C. Rice

Text and art copyright by David C. Rice, 2025

Just Keep Walking Press, Berkeley, California, 2025

Contact: davidrice13131@gmail.com

ISBN: 978-1-7331154-4-5

for Amanda — 1969-2023

for Snag Lake, Lassen Volcanic National Park

for Ariel and Ezra

After The End is a poetic lament, a meditation on loss, grief, sorrow, and the search for hope. Through tanka poems and tanka prose, David C. Rice focuses on the loss of his mother, his daughter's passing, the destruction of most of the Lassen Volcanic National Park during the Dixie Fire . . . and the looming climate crisis plaguing the world.

There is a sense of nostalgic fervor to these poetic narratives that adds to the rich and emotionally powerful themes . . . All in all, it was an inspiring read for me. If you're a poetry lover, I can't recommend this book highly enough.

Pikasho Deka, Readers' Favorite, 5-star review

dark early
solstice soon
I rotate
around her sun
in an endless orbit

late afternoon
fall silence
if we could start over
I'd start with birdsong
and humility

TABLE OF CONTENTS

FLIPPED – PART ONE

FLIPPED – PART TWO

FLIPPED— PART I

Gentle Sorrow

mom
didn't want to live
to be a hundred
wish her wish
had not been granted

deleting photos
from my phone
a sunset . . . a sunset . . .
I should have taken
more pictures of mom

seventy-two hours
since mom died
an owl hoots, hoot, hoots
closer, closer . . .
did she just say *goodbye*?

we open the bag
by the birch she planted
spread her ashes—
my daughter tells me
to take more vitamins

Monday morning
mom still gone
appointments to keep
I tighten the bolts
on another day

for the last time
I walk up the driveway
she had repaired last year—
my inheritance
just keep going

my daughter takes
the small ceramic duck
from mom's house
what will she keep
of mine?

Rupture

again . . . *my daughter died . . .*
sunk in her dementia
my friend surfaces
you never lose
the ones you've lost

an old woman
walking with a cane
if you'd lived
I bet you'd have worn
that lavender jacket

don't want to phone
just to hear her voice . . .
I used to know
she was calling
just before she did

tires checked
cooler, tents, flashlights
check, check, check
and the box of ashes —
her last camping trip

she said she'd scatter
my ashes
at that mountain lake
now I'm going to hike there
with hers

today
at the market
where I don't buy lettuce
for her anymore ...
I almost forgot

a tree
she will never see
just leafing out
never thought spring
would make me sad

Unraveling Grief

Liminal

When your daughter dies, the past pulls you back. She had dessert for breakfast on the solstice. She called to talk as she drove home from work. The experts say it's grief, and it will lessen. They know more than me, but when your daughter dies, you don't want your grief to lessen. That's where she lives now.

> new willow leaves
> the pale green of promise
> I'll always wonder
> how she would have finished
> her self-portrait

And Then the Days

homemade cobbler
from our berry patch
she's not here
to proclaim
it's the best one yet

You have your daily routines. The usual breakfast, the bedtime ritual. But when your daughter dies, those buttons snap, and your routines no longer contain you. Unenlightened, you chop wood and carry water. Enlightened, you chop wood and carry water. When your daughter dies, you chop wood and chop water. When your daughter dies, your routines are cotton shirts in cold rain that don't keep you warm. The safety of the familiar becomes the annoyance of repetition. You want, well, what you want you can't have, and what you have you don't want.

wind
carries blackbird song
across the meadow
I throw my dirge
as high as I can

Stuck

some spring
I won't see
these blossoms either
she just didn't get
to say goodbye

If the oft-repeated cliché "be here now," is not so obvious as to be inaudible, maybe some people hear the reminder and change their behavior. But how can I "be here now"? My daily wish that my daughter hadn't died before me will never change. If I stop grieving, I'll lose her again.

parents watch kids
cross the street to school—
the future looks brighter
if your child
is still here

No Safe Place

When you tell people you know, but who don't know your daughter died, they touch your arm. You thank them. You know they're thinking, beyond their genuine empathy, they are so glad that didn't happen to their daughter. As you would if you were them. When they touch your arm it helps, momentarily. You try to hold onto those moments . . .

> a feather on the trail
> not on a wing
> —that's natural, too—
> I keep walking . . .
> flight beyond me

Poem Medicine

"You have to let go of the life you have to accept the life you've been given." Got it. Then my fifty-three-year-old daughter had a brain hemorrhage and died.

if you need anything . . .
I need to wake up
by a river
with her asleep
in her tent . . .

I hadn't understood at all: the phone call, the hospital, the "there's nothing we can do."

mid-summer heat
flowers and grasses
going to seed
next spring
she'll still be gone

Down to Earth

after the fire
a woodpecker hammers . . .
it takes
a long time
to rebuild a forest

To get our attention, we need a loud, incessant screech or a visual double-take. A burned forest will work. The shadow of a still-standing-climate-burnt tree looked like a person to me, until I realized I was not looking at a tree, but my shadow. "Sorry," I said. Just blurted it out. Felt a little silly, talking to a tree, but then I had been talking to my daughter all morning, and she wasn't even here.

scattered her ashes
around the stump
of a once huge pine
we first saw together—
thought about not leaving

No End

I'm keeping the space
you once filled
open—
don't want to go on
without your light

On our first backpack trip together, I carried my daughter— nine-months-old—on my back. On our next trip, when she was seven, she carried her sleeping bag and the candy bars. When she was grown, we hiked in the Sierra.

The day after we went to a restaurant to honor what would have been her fifty-fifth birthday, I was surprised to feel relieved. Hadn't realized I'd been carrying an increasingly heavy pack full of missing-her the past few weeks. Not sure how to lighten my load next year, though. How could I leave her behind on her birthday?

madsad
—why isn't that a word?—
I don't need trail markers
to follow
my tears

On and On

It's been a year-and-a-half since my daughter died.
Sitting in my room, I see the picture I painted of her and
the past pulls me back. When I'm reading or vacuuming
now, though, she doesn't claim my attention as much as
she did just after she died. I realize this is how normal
grieving is supposed to go, yet getting used to her not
being here makes me sad all over again.

woke up
counted the weeks
my daughter's been gone . . .
don't want to let
the past pass

Nothing Else To Do

Each night I hope to dream of you.

I want to know how you're doing or, perhaps more accurately, I want to escape my repetitive, daytime, moody thoughts and feelings, even if your night visit would be ephemeral. One night you called and were sad for us. All I could do was nod. One night you showed up and just stood there. I woke up ecstatic, then bereft.

Each night I hope to dream of you.

> mind spinning
> I land on
> you're-not-here
> now I can't move
> for ten thousand turns

FLIPPED— PART 2

Summer Idyll

dark and no wind
at our backpack camp
my breath
in sync
with the creek thrum

warblers in the willows
an eagle in a pine
that night I dreamed in color
and woke
on top of a tree

mountain dawn
here comes the sky
mauve with a hint of pink
when the trees turn green
bird time!

I lean against the pine
and watch birds
in the willows
—fourth decade now—
calmed by continuity

foot-high golden grass
ripples in the wind . . .
if I were tiny
I could hold on
to a stem

mountain meadow
moonlight
silvers the grass
suddenly . . .
I'm moonlit, too

Thud

fallen branchlets
swatch the ground brown
I pick one up
fire-scorched needles
blanket my hand

in the photo
chiaroscuro trees and shadows
trying to imagine
shades of green
before the fire

we'd watch warblers
drink beneath a willow
ten feet away
I need to remember
what's not here

a fire ring
I remember
when we could protect
the forest . . .
shadows of burnt trees

searching for places
to pitch our tents
where a tree won't fall
hard to sleep well
in a graveyard

hundreds of frogs
in the meadow that year
—we walked carefully—
now all we see
are our bootprints

lake dusk-calm
if I stay up
with the ghost trees
stars will remind me
time has no end

Unraveling Hope

Hard to See

an historical plaque
on a bare hill—
here stood the tree
where a pine marten
took the chickadee chicks

Looking back with binoculars can magnify time's changes: that green forest where you played capture-the-flag as a kid is now a forest floor of criss-crossed fallen logs with no place to hide. That blue, tree-ringed mountain lake is now a blue tub surrounded by bare, ashy soil. You focus the knob on today: chainsawed-stumps tomb a hillside.

sunlight glints off
the burnt bark
of the one standing pine
I should embrace it
and smudge myself

Legacy

You want kids to have the chance to paint their own pictures. First crayons: draw a rainbow. Then colored pencils, pastels, brushes (!). Show them how to mix yellows and blues to make greens. "Paint what you see."

They see a fire-mowed forest. They're mixing all the primary colors to make muddy gray. There's no pot of gold at the end of an ashy rainbow.

> missing pieces
> in the jigsaw puzzle . . .
> finished the blue lake
> no greens
> for the forest

Life Cycles

The young may exaggerate. Their pre-frontal cortexes are dough, not bread. But they understand, when the adults-in-charge make decisions to keep the financial engines running smoothly, even though the climate alarm keeps buzzing, that those adults are smash-trashing their future.

The young have to keep pushing, even if they're not fully formed.

> the cranes
> were still calling
> when we left—
> how else could they try
> to tell us . . .

Next Gen

trying to blend
the scurrying quail
with this drought-wrapped hill . . .
my frayed brushes
just make a muddle

Your English teacher gives you words: *exonerate,*
torpor. Learn their meaning. Use them in a sentence. There
is no way to exonerate human beings who sink into torpor
as the temperature rises. *Esoteric, burnish.* An esoteric
cadre has access to the climate-change tool box, but they
deludedly think they are burnishing their power-
credentials by continuing to burn the earth.

Climate-savvy teens *proselytize* at the mall. Maybe
we need to join them in grieving our future because, if not
grief, what else can open the lock and let us out of
ourselves?

after the fire
black bark
needleless . . . silent
nothing here
to replenish me

Lights Out

Some songbirds migrate at night, and ornithologists can record their calls, analyze the sonograms, and figure out what species are flying in the dark above our heads each spring and fall. Neat, right—but what are they saying? Either Watch out for the night lights" or "Why do humans make this so hard?"

hearing aids died
no bird
is calling to me—
wonder if the future
will amplify this silence

Back in Line

For forty years, we camped by the creek even though, for the last three years, putting up our tents was risky because of the fire—most of the dead trees had not yet fallen. This year, we safely camped on the other side of the lake, under some huge red firs that have not burned. We walked to get our water, seeing birds along the way.

I wish I could say I'd moved from denial to the acceptance stage of grieving for the forest that used-to-be but, looking across the lake at the dark wooden spires, I knew I was too old to live long enough to see any new seedlings grow tall here, and I'd never see the forest green again.

Then a peregrine rushes past.

> I toss
> a burnt stick
> in the sunlit rapids . . .
> it disappears
> I toss another

Congress of the Parties —Hope

Group A

As the fires burned, the droughts parched, and the earth kept careening through a climate calamity, the orthodox working group studied the wisdom of the past and cited hope as essential to help us get through the crisis. "To live without hope is to cease to live" (Dostoyevsky). "'Hope' is the thing with feathers--/that perches on the soul--" (Dickinson). We must act with hope, they said, because without hope, we will not act.

> chalk art
> on the sidewalk
> —kids' petunias—
> when it rains
> the smudges will still inspire

Congress of the Parties—Hope

Group B

The apostate working group saw hope as helpful but non-essential in dealing with the climate crisis and the solastalgia epidemic. Hope is not a plan, they said. To hope may be human, but to lose hope is human, too. We may breathe hope, but the air is getting worse.

a thrush
then two more
none last week
we're migrating, too
just not sure where

Congress of the Parties—Hope

Group C

The third working group, beyond hope, argued hope was not capable of helping us through the climate crisis. "Giving up on hope is what leads to action" (Jensen). Hope will not help us help the earth, they said, and besides, losing species is just what the earth has always done. Hope is an empty packet of seeds, and it doesn't rain here anymore anyway. The Buddhists had it right: "all things in cyclic existence are transient, impermanent." Grief, to help us accept our limitations, would be more helpful than hope now.

> extreme fire danger
> woodland road widened
> in preparation . . .
> if the trees do burn
> they'll decompose

Connected

a crane calls once
and lands near the lake
the sun
on the burnt trees
brightens

Discouraged is easy. Look at the fire-blackened willow limbs. Mastedon skeletons, someone said. But the next year, green shoots. The roots are still alive. The willow will green again.

Courage, which the eco-activists say we need now, is hard. But we do have connections. We could mix ourselves together and make a new shade of green.

the one willow left
in the fire-scarred meadow
hosts a flycatcher . . .
enough
to encourage me

IN LINE

Future Tripping

Odd, this desire to be remembered. My friends will remember me, but many of them will likely die soon after I do, if not before. My grandchildren will remember me, but their children, if they have children, won't. After seven generations, even my DNA will be gone. Maybe being remembered isn't quite the point. Besides, I'm privileged to have enough money to afford good health care, don't live in a war zone, and might well live past my life expectancy; wanting more seems greedy.

Still, it would have been comforting to know my daughter was still here, remembering me after I'm gone, at least for a few decades. *Intangible immortality* my friend said. Of course, after I die, I won't know if I'm remembered or not, but feelings aren't rational.

> the fallen pine
> where I scattered her ashes . . .
> hope her kids
> will hike here
> with mine

Root Bound

Her dying made me think about what I wanted to do before I died, and my bucket list has changed. Now it's be here for her children, my grandchildren, maybe see a few more birds; well, maybe that trip to Italy to see some old masters . . .

And plant a tree in her memory. Only a few people would know it was her tree, but there would be a place— not just inside us— to go and remember her. She would have planted trees if she had lived. Now, she'll still be helping the earth breathe.

> second missed birthday . . .
> to fill this hole
> I'll root
> a redwood seedling . . .
> it could live for centuries

Choose Wisely

With my daughter gone, to whom do I bequeath my stuff? Friends won't want my baby pictures or mom's glass penguin. My grandchildren might live into the next century, but they won't want to cart that glass penguin around for seventy-five years. My daughter would have kept that penguin.

Well, after I'm gone, along with the box of ashes, why not a box of my stuff? Suppose there were museums, not just for famous people, that displayed boxes of ordinary people's stuff. Visitors could come see what each of us thought was important, personal time capsules. I'd like to leave a bit of myself behind; I bet other people would, too.

It will be necessary to limit the size of the box.

> for seventy years
> I played this violin
> when I'm gone
> put those notes in a bottle
> pop the cork on my birthday

Making Do

My daughter and I didn't get to say goodbye. The rope broke. My frayed feelings are a continual reminder of what we lost. The other people I love? I want to say goodbye to them; I'd like them to say goodbye to me. I'd like to double-knot our life-lines before we have to leave each other.

I did kiss her before I left the hospital, where she lay, waiting to be an organ donor. I said goodbye, but she couldn't, so we didn't.

> a kid chatters
> to her dad
> —links in a chain—
> neither thinking
> it could ever snap

Daily Practice

Her premature death spotlighted my own death-thoughts. I don't mean getting my will and trust in order. I mean thinking about not being here. We all try to obey the be-here-now commandment, but my mind wanders back to my daughter. Yes, bodies wear out, but her body just crashed one day, and she was something of a health nut. Am I going to crash one day? What about the people I love? Short, pain-free deaths? Long, painful deaths? Dementia? I re-direct. And what about the climate-calamity horror series we're all watching? How will it end? The mind wanders. I re-direct.

> walking through my life
> footsteps in the fog . . .
> the uncrossable river
> of my daughter's death . . .
> then a rainbow sunset

SIGNS

large flowers
orange, yellow, pink
falling from a tree
in perfect shape—
there she is again

an accipiter
rushed down the trail
I ducked . . .
how else could it warn me
take another path

everyday
a hummingbird visits
our sage
I talk to her
as if she's you

dewdrops
on a spider's web
I'm trying
to catch and release
loss

is that her
in the slow-moving stream
where we scattered her ashes?
two years ago
—I'm not leaving

Visible

We went to the fabric store. She was going to make me a quilt. I picked my colors, and she cut and sewed four squares together: a blue-streaked ochre center surrounded by patterned cerulean blue and Payne's Gray triangles. I taped it to a wall in my room. Yes!

Then she died.

When we cleared out her house, I took the fabric and put it in a box in my closet. Eighteen months later, able to touch it again, I decided to ask someone to copy the pattern and make a wall hanging for me, but where to hang it? My wife suggested on the door to my study. Perfect!

> each morning
> I unclasp the day
> and put it on . . .
> she's waiting
> in the next room

Back-and-Forth

Peeling, lead-based . . . I had her house painted. She was going to do it. Now I don't recognize the spring-green exterior with spiffy, tan trim, as the place she lived. It's as if I helped her disappear.

The pictures of her on my phone don't help. They just make me wonder how she would have grayed. I did paint the photograph on her memorial brochure. She's standing among trees, hands on her hips, smiling. Wish I could have given it to her.

first big storm
wet leaves slick the sidewalk
wearing
her green rain jacket
keeps me dry

Kid Gloves

One afternoon, on the sidewalk of a small street with food shops, a little girl, maybe three-years-old, was walking with her mother, holding her hand. As they passed, the girl let go and extended both her hands toward me. I took her hands in mine. She smiled. The mother, smiling but looking slightly unnerved, said, "Maybe she knew you in a past life," before nudging the girl to let go. As the mother and girl walked away, the girl looked back at me.

kid's gardening gloves
in the basement
after my daughter died
where is the girl
whose hands they'll fit?

After The End

she showed up
in a dream last night
as if nothing had happened . . .
I need to widen
my field of view

The winter solstice—light returning, start of the
real new year unencumbered by religious or secular
holidays—was our favorite day. It's going on two years
now since she died; I don't see her light coming back. But
maybe her light is not coming back, because she never
completely left. Maybe she just changed her shape.

a barn swallow
hovers at eye level
my friend and I both say
that's her
wonder when she'll visit next

morning dew
on the persimmon tree . . .
I touch one
and it disappears—
she's everywhere

Acknowledgments

I am grateful to the little magazines and online journals that published the following poems: *Contemporary Haibun Online*—Life Cycles; *Contemporary Haibun 20*—And Then the Days; *red lights*—again . . . my daughter died, today, a tree; *gusts*—don't want to phone, deleting photos, she said she'd scatter; *International Tanka*—Hard to See, no safe place; *Ribbons*—And Then the Days, Down to Earth, mom, hearing aids died, she takes, missing pieces, a kid chatters, everyday; *Tanka Society of America Members' Anthology*—a barn swallow, tires checked; *the art of tanka* —in the photo, late afternoon; *Triveni*—new willow leaves, Poem Medicine, Connected.

I would like to thank my wife, Carol Shattuck-Rice, always my first reader; Amanda's friend, Deb Cohan; Pamela Daniels and Noreen Linden, who helped with the cover; and, especially, Autumn Noelle Hall, for their help with earlier drafts of these poems.

Also, thank you to Susan Weaver for copyediting.

Amanda Abarbanel-Rice graduated from Berkeley High School and Wesleyan University. She received a masters in teaching degree from the New School in San Francisco and taught elementary school in the Berkeley Unified School District for twenty five years. She had two children, (Ariel and Ezra), was an outdoor enthusiast (river rafting, car camping, backpacking), a reader, and a quilter.

Snag Lake is located in the eastern part of Lassen Volcanic National Park in northern California. I co-led an Audubon backpack-birding trip to Snag Lake for forty years. The 2021 Dixie Fire burned two-thirds of the park, including most of the forest around Snag Lake.